The AI 2.0 Report: How it will change your Worlds Economy and Wealth Potential

Creating a report on how AI 2.0 will change the world, its impact on people's lives, and its potential to become a $25 - $50 trillion industry is a comprehensive project. To ensure we address this topic thoroughly and effectively, let's break down the process into manageable steps:

1. Understanding Requirements and Audience: First, let's clarify the intended use of this report. Who is the target audience? What specific aspects of AI 2.0 are most relevant to them? The tone

and level of detail will vary significantly depending on whether we're addressing industry professionals, policymakers, academics, or the general public. allocation. This will help ensure we cover all necessary topics and maintain a clear structure throughout the report.

2. Section-by-Section Writing: We'll tackle the report one section at a time,

 starting with an introduction to AI 2.0 and its foundational technologies. Following sections will explore specific changes AI 2.0 is expected to bring, its implications for various industries, ethical considerations, and its economic potential. Each section will be written and delivered sequentially, allowing for feedback and adjustments along the way.

3. Incorporating Data and Case Studies: To strengthen the report, we'll include relevant data, trends, and case studies demonstrating AI 2.0's impact and potential. This will provide evidence to support our analysis and projections.

4.Conclusion and Recommendations: The final sections will summarize the report's key points and offer recommendations for stakeholders in leveraging AI 2.0's potential responsibly and effectively.

5. Formatting and References: The report will be formatted with proper citations and references to all sources used. This ensures the credibility and reliability of the information presented.

Proposed Outline for the Report

Introduction

- Overview of AI 2.0: Definition, evolution from AI 1.0, and key technologies.

- Purpose and scope of the report.

Foundations of AI 2.0

- Key technologies and methodologies driving AI 2.0.

- Advances in machine learning, natural language processing, and computer vision.

- Role of big data and computing power.

Impact on Industries

- Healthcare: Personalized medicine, diagnostics, and treatment.

- Finance: Automated trading, fraud detection, and personalized banking.

- Manufacturing: Automation, predictive maintenance, and supply chain optimization.

- Transportation: Autonomous vehicles and logistics improvements.

- Other key sectors.

Societal Implications

- Employment: Job displacement and creation.

- Privacy and Security: Data protection challenges and cybersecurity.

- Ethical Considerations: Bias, fairness, and decision-making.

- Global Inequalities: Bridging or widening the digital divide.

Economic Potential

- Analysis of the $100 trillion projection: Assumptions, drivers, and challenges.

- Comparison with the economic impact of previous technological revolutions.

- Investment trends and future outlook.

Challenges and Solutions

- Technical hurdles: Scalability, reliability, and efficiency.
- Regulatory and policy considerations.
- Collaboration between stakeholders: Governments, industry, academia, and civil society.

Conclusion and Recommendations

- Summary of key findings.

- Strategic recommendations for various stakeholders.

- The future of AI 2.0 and ongoing research directions.

References

Great, let's proceed with the first section of the report, focusing on the Introduction to AI 2.0. This section will lay the foundation for the entire report by defining AI 2.0, outlining its evolution from AI 1.0, and highlighting the significance of this technology in today's world.

Introduction to AI 2.0

Overview of AI 2.0

Artificial Intelligence (AI) 2.0 represents a transformative leap in the capabilities and applications of AI technologies. Unlike its predecessor, AI 1.0, which primarily focused on narrow tasks and rule-based systems, AI 2.0 encompasses advanced machine learning algorithms, deep learning networks, and big data analytics to enable systems that can learn, adapt, and make decisions with minimal human intervention. This evolution marks a shift towards more generalized AI that can perform a wide range of tasks, mimic human-like understanding, and generate innovative solutions to complex problems.

Evolution from AI 1.0 to AI 2.0

The transition from AI 1.0 to AI 2.0 has been driven by significant advancements in computing power, data availability, and algorithmic innovation. AI 1.0 systems were often limited by their reliance on explicit programming and lack of adaptability, making them suitable for specific tasks such as basic customer service interactions, simple decision-making processes, and structured data analysis. In contrast, AI 2.0 technologies leverage the vast amounts of data generated in the digital age, along with powerful computational resources, to develop self-learning systems capable of deep understanding and reasoning. This shift has enabled breakthroughs in natural language processing, computer vision, and autonomous decision-making, paving the way for

applications that were once considered science fiction.

The Significance of AI 2.0

AI 2.0 is set to revolutionize how we live, work, and interact with the world around us. Its impact extends far beyond technological innovation, promising to reshape industries, redefine productivity, and create new economic opportunities. Moreover, AI 2.0 has the potential to address some of the most pressing challenges facing humanity, including healthcare diagnostics, climate change, and resource optimization. However, alongside these opportunities come significant ethical, societal, and security challenges that must be navigated thoughtfully to ensure that the benefits of AI 2.0 are realized equitably and responsibly.

This introduction sets the stage for a deeper exploration of AI 2.0's foundational technologies, its impacts across various sectors, and the broader implications for society and the global economy. In the following sections, we'll delve into the specifics of how AI 2.0 is shaping the future and examine the factors contributing to its projected economic value.

Moving forward, we'll delve into the Foundations of AI 2.0 section. This part of the report will cover the core technologies and methodologies that underpin AI 2.0, highlighting how advances in these areas have catalyzed the transition from AI 1.0 to AI 2.0 and set the stage for unprecedented applications and impacts across various domains.

Foundations of AI 2.0

AI 2.0 is built on a foundation of cutting-edge technologies and methodologies that enable machines to learn from data, adapt to new situations, and perform complex tasks. At the heart of AI 2.0 are three key components: machine learning algorithms, deep learning networks, and big data analytics. These components work in tandem to create systems capable of self-improvement and decision-making with levels of sophistication previously unattainable.

Key Technologies and Methodologies

• Machine Learning Algorithms: Machine learning represents a core technology of AI 2.0, enabling computers to learn from and make predictions or decisions based on data. Unlike traditional programming, which requires explicit instructions for every decision, machine learning algorithms allow systems to learn patterns and insights directly from data, improving their accuracy and effectiveness over time.

• Deep Learning Networks: A subset of machine learning, deep learning utilizes neural networks with many layers (hence "deep") to model complex patterns in data. Deep learning has been pivotal in achieving breakthroughs in areas such as natural language processing (NLP), computer vision, and speech recognition. These networks mimic the way the human brain operates, allowing machines to process and interpret vast amounts of data in ways similar to humans.

- Big Data Analytics: The explosion of data in the digital era has provided the fuel for AI 2.0's advancement. Big data analytics involves the processing and analysis of vast datasets to uncover patterns, trends, and correlations. This capability is crucial for training AI models, enabling them to learn from a broader range of examples and perform more accurately and effectively in real-world applications.

Advances in Machine Learning, Natural Language Processing, and Computer Vision

- Machine Learning Advances: The development of more sophisticated algorithms, including reinforcement learning and generative adversarial networks (GANs), has expanded the scope and efficiency of machine learning. These advances allow for more complex simulations, creative content generation, and improved decision-making capabilities.

- Natural Language Processing (NLP): NLP has seen significant advancements due to deep learning, enabling machines to understand, interpret, and generate human language with increasing accuracy. Applications include translation services, sentiment analysis, and conversational agents that can understand and respond to human queries naturally.

- Computer Vision: AI 2.0 has dramatically improved the capabilities of computer vision, allowing systems to recognize, interpret, and react to visual data with high precision. This has enabled applications such as autonomous vehicles, facial recognition systems, and advanced surveillance technologies.

Role of Big Data and Computing Power

The synergistic relationship between big data and computing power is a critical enabler of AI 2.0. The availability of large datasets provides the raw material for training increasingly sophisticated AI models, while advances in computing power, including GPUs and cloud computing, allow these data-intensive models to be trained and run efficiently. This combination has accelerated the pace of innovation in AI, making technologies like real-time language translation, self-driving cars, and personalized medicine feasible.

This exploration of the foundations of AI 2.0 underscores the technological innovations driving this new era of artificial intelligence. As we progress into the subsequent sections of the report, these foundational elements will provide the basis for understanding AI 2.0's transformative potential across various industries and societal domains.

Great, let's move on to the Impact on Industries section. This segment of the report will explore how AI 2.0 technologies are revolutionizing various sectors, including healthcare, finance, manufacturing, transportation, and more. We'll look at specific applications, the benefits they bring, and the challenges they pose.

Impact on Industries

AI 2.0 is set to revolutionize industries by enhancing efficiency, enabling innovation, and creating new opportunities for growth. Its impact is wide-ranging, affecting sectors from healthcare to finance, and from manufacturing to transportation.

Healthcare: Personalized Medicine, Diagnostics, and Treatment

- Personalized Medicine: AI 2.0 enables the analysis of vast datasets of genetic information, leading to personalized treatment plans that are more effective and have fewer side effects.

- Diagnostics: Machine learning models can now outperform human experts in diagnosing diseases from images, such as X-rays and MRIs, leading to faster and more accurate diagnoses.

- Treatment: AI-driven robots assist in surgeries with precision beyond human capabilities, and AI systems help in drug discovery by predicting the effectiveness of compounds more efficiently.

Finance: Automated Trading, Fraud Detection, and Personalized Banking

- **Automated Trading:** AI algorithms can analyze market data in real time to make automated trading decisions, potentially increasing returns and reducing risks.

- **Fraud Detection:** AI systems are capable of detecting patterns indicative of fraudulent activities, thereby enhancing the security of financial transactions.

- **Personalized Banking:** Banks use AI to offer personalized financial advice and optimize customer service, improving the overall banking experience.

Manufacturing: Automation, Predictive Maintenance, and Supply Chain Optimization

- **Automation:** AI-driven robots are increasingly used in manufacturing for tasks that require precision and consistency, leading to higher productivity and safety.
- **Predictive Maintenance:** By analyzing data from machinery, AI can

predict failures before they happen, reducing downtime and maintenance costs.

•	Supply Chain Optimization: AI algorithms optimize supply chains by predicting demand, managing inventory, and identifying the most efficient logistics routes.

Transportation: Autonomous Vehicles and Logistics Improvements

•	Autonomous Vehicles: AI is at the core of developing self-driving cars, which promise to improve safety, reduce traffic congestion, and transform urban mobility.

- Logistics Improvements: AI applications in logistics can optimize routing, improve delivery times, and reduce costs, thereby enhancing the efficiency of transportation networks.

AI 2.0's impact on these industries demonstrates the vast potential of this technology to transform the way businesses operate and serve their customers. However, it also presents challenges, including the need for significant investment in technology, the potential for job displacement, and ethical considerations related to privacy and decision-making.

As we delve further into the societal implications and the broader economic potential of AI 2.0 in the following sections, these industry examples will serve as a backdrop for understanding the multifaceted impact of AI on our world.

Focusing specifically on the impact of AI 2.0 on the stock market within the Finance industry section provides an intriguing angle. AI 2.0 technologies, with their advanced machine learning algorithms and big data analytics capabilities, are significantly transforming stock market operations, trading strategies, and investment analysis. Here's a deeper dive into how AI 2.0 is reshaping the stock market landscape.

Impact of AI 2.0 on the Stock Market

Automated Trading and Algorithmic Strategies

AI 2.0 technologies have revolutionized trading strategies through the development of sophisticated automated trading systems. These systems use machine learning algorithms to analyze vast amounts of market data in real-time, identifying patterns and trends that are imperceptible to human traders. By processing this information, AI-driven platforms can execute trades at optimal times, maximizing profits and minimizing losses. Moreover, algorithmic trading strategies can adapt to new market conditions as they evolve, continuously learning and improving their decision-making processes.

Enhanced Market Analysis and Prediction

One of the most significant impacts of AI 2.0 on the stock market is its ability to enhance market analysis and prediction. By leveraging deep learning networks, AI systems can analyze not just structured data, like stock prices and financial reports, but also unstructured data, such as news articles, social media posts, and economic forecasts. This comprehensive analysis enables more accurate predictions of market movements, stock performance, and even the potential impact of geopolitical events on financial markets. As a result, investors and analysts equipped with AI tools can make more informed decisions, reducing the risk associated with investments.

Risk Management and Fraud Detection

AI 2.0 plays a crucial role in risk management by identifying potential risks and anomalies that could indicate fraudulent activity. Through the analysis of transaction patterns and behaviors, AI systems can detect irregularities that deviate from the norm, signaling possible fraud. This capability is vital for regulatory compliance and for maintaining the integrity of financial markets. Additionally, AI-driven risk management tools help investors assess the risk profile of their portfolios, suggesting adjustments to align with their risk tolerance and investment goals.

Personalized Investment Services

AI 2.0 technologies are also democratizing access to personalized investment advice, previously available only to high-net-worth individuals. Robo-advisors, powered by AI algorithms, provide customized investment recommendations based on an individual's financial goals, risk tolerance, and time horizon. These platforms can automatically adjust portfolios in response to changing market conditions, ensuring optimal asset allocation at all times. The scalability and efficiency of AI-driven investment services are making sophisticated financial advice more accessible to a broader audience.

The intersection of AI 2.0 and the stock market represents a paradigm shift in how financial markets operate, offering enhanced efficiency, improved accuracy in predictions, and personalized investment solutions. However, this transformation also raises questions about market volatility, the ethical implications of automated trading, and the **Need for regulatory frameworks to manage these advanced technologies.**

As we move to explore the societal implications of AI 2.0, the considerations surrounding the stock market and finance sector will serve as a critical example of the broader challenges and opportunities presented by the integration of AI into our economic systems.

Continuing with the report, we'll explore the Societal Implications of AI 2.0. This section examines how the widespread adoption of AI 2.0 technologies influences employment, privacy, security, ethical considerations, and global inequalities. By addressing these topics, we aim to understand the broader impact of AI 2.0 on society and the challenges that accompany its benefits.

Societal Implications of AI 2.0

Employment: Job Displacement and Creation

The integration of AI 2.0 technologies into various industries is significantly impacting the workforce. While AI systems can increase efficiency and productivity, they also pose a risk of job displacement for roles that are routine and predictable. However, AI also creates opportunities for job creation in sectors where human-AI collaboration is critical. The challenge lies in managing the transition, including retraining workers and developing skills that complement AI technologies.

Privacy and Security: Data Protection Challenges and Cybersecurity

As AI 2.0 technologies rely heavily on data, they raise significant privacy and security concerns. The collection, storage, and analysis of vast amounts of personal information present risks of data breaches and misuse. Moreover, AI systems themselves can become targets of cyberattacks, potentially leading to the manipulation of automated processes. Ensuring robust cybersecurity measures and ethical data handling practices is paramount to maintaining trust in AI technologies.

Ethical Considerations: Bias, Fairness, and Decision-Making

AI systems are only as unbiased as the data they are trained on. Historical data can contain inherent biases, which AI algorithms can inadvertently perpetuate. Addressing these issues requires careful design and continuous monitoring of AI systems to ensure fairness and transparency in decision-making processes. Ethical considerations also extend to the autonomy of AI decisions, raising questions about accountability and the role of human oversight.

Global Inequalities: Bridging or Widening the Digital Divide

AI 2.0 has the potential to significantly improve living standards and address challenges such as healthcare access, education, and economic development. However, there's a risk that these benefits might not be evenly distributed, potentially widening the gap between technologically advanced nations and those with limited access to digital infrastructure. Ensuring inclusive growth and international cooperation is crucial to leveraging AI for global good.

The societal implications of AI 2.0 are complex and multifaceted. While AI presents unprecedented opportunities for advancement and problem-solving, it also introduces challenges that require thoughtful consideration and action from policymakers, technologists, and society at large. Addressing these issues collaboratively is essential to ensure that the benefits of AI 2.0 are realized equitably and responsibly across the globe.

As we proceed to the next section on the Economic Potential of AI 2.0, we'll explore how these societal implications intersect with the technology's capacity to drive economic growth and innovation.

Now, we'll transition to discussing the Economic Potential of AI 2.0. This section will explore the factors contributing to AI 2.0's projected impact as a $100 trillion industry, examining its potential to drive growth, innovation, and productivity across the global economy. We'll also consider the investment trends and challenges that accompany this forecast.

Economic Potential of AI 2.0

AI 2.0 stands at the forefront of the next wave of economic transformation, with the potential to reshape industries, enhance productivity, and spawn new markets.

Its economic impact is expected to be profound, influencing both the macroeconomic landscape and the microeconomic dynamics of businesses and labor markets.

Analysis of the $100 Trillion Projection

The projection of AI 2.0 as a $100 trillion industry is grounded in its capacity to drive significant gains in efficiency, innovation, and new product and service creation. AI 2.0 technologies can optimize operations, reduce waste, personalize products and services, and solve complex problems, leading to substantial economic value. Key factors contributing to this projection include:

- Productivity Gains: AI 2.0 can automate routine tasks, analyze data more efficiently than humans, and optimize production processes, leading to significant productivity improvements.

- Innovation and New Markets: AI 2.0 enables the development of new technologies, products, and services, creating entirely new markets and revenue streams. Examples include personalized medicine, autonomous transportation, and AI-driven financial services.

- Global Efficiency: By improving supply chain management, energy consumption, and resource allocation, AI 2.0 can enhance global economic efficiency, contributing to sustainability and reducing costs.

Investment Trends and Future Outlook

Investment in AI 2.0 technologies has been growing rapidly, with venture capital, corporate funding, and government initiatives supporting research, development, and deployment. The competitive advantage gained through AI adoption is driving businesses to allocate substantial resources to AI projects. Furthermore, public-private partnerships are emerging as a strategy to accelerate AI innovation and adoption, addressing societal challenges such as healthcare and climate change.

However, realizing AI 2.0's economic potential requires overcoming challenges related to data privacy, ethical AI use, and ensuring inclusive benefits. Additionally, the transition may disrupt labor markets, necessitating policies that support workforce adaptation and retraining.

Comparison with Previous Technological Revolutions

The impact of AI 2.0 can be compared to previous technological revolutions, such as the Industrial Revolution and the Information Technology Revolution. While each revolution brought about significant economic shifts and challenges, AI 2.0 is unique in its speed, scope, and the depth of its potential impacts. The integration of AI across all sectors and its ability to enhance human capabilities distinguish it as a pivotal force in shaping the future economy.

The economic potential of AI 2.0 is vast, promising to catalyze a new era of growth, innovation, and efficiency. As we navigate the path toward realizing this potential, it will be crucial to address the accompanying challenges and ensure that the benefits of AI 2.0 are shared broadly across societies.

In the following sections, we will delve into the challenges and solutions associated with harnessing AI 2.0's economic potential, as well as strategic recommendations for stakeholders.

Transitioning to the Challenges and Solutions segment, we delve into the multifaceted obstacles that come with the widespread adoption and integration of AI 2.0 technologies. This exploration will include technical hurdles, regulatory considerations, and the collaborative effort required among stakeholders to harness AI 2.0's full potential responsibly and effectively.

Challenges and Solutions Associated with AI 2.0

Technical Hurdles: Scalability, Reliability, and Efficiency

- Scalability: As AI systems grow in complexity, scaling them while maintaining performance and managing costs becomes a challenge. Solutions include investing in cloud infrastructure, developing more efficient algorithms, and adopting federated learning approaches that allow AI models to learn from decentralized data sources.

- Reliability: Ensuring AI systems operate reliably under varied and unforeseen conditions is crucial, especially in critical applications like healthcare and autonomous transportation. Developing robust testing frameworks, incorporating extensive validation datasets, and using simulation environments can enhance reliability.

- Efficiency: The energy consumption of training large AI models poses sustainability concerns. Solutions involve designing more energy-efficient computing hardware, optimizing algorithms for better performance with lower resource requirements, and adopting green AI practices.

Regulatory and Policy Considerations

• Data Privacy and Protection: Implementing regulations that protect individual privacy while not stifling innovation is a balancing act. Solutions include developing privacy-enhancing technologies, such as differential privacy and secure multi-party computation, and establishing clear, globally harmonized data protection standards.

- Ethical AI Use: Developing guidelines and frameworks for ethical AI use is essential to address biases, ensure transparency, and maintain human oversight. Initiatives like AI ethics boards within organizations and industry-wide standards can guide responsible AI development and deployment.

- Inclusive Benefits: To prevent widening the digital divide, policies should aim at equitable access to AI technologies. Solutions include public investment in digital infrastructure, education and retraining programs, and fostering inclusive innovation ecosystems.

Collaboration between Stakeholders: Governments, Industry, Academia, and Civil Society

- Public-Private Partnerships: Collaborations between governments and private sector entities can accelerate the development and ethical deployment of AI technologies, particularly in addressing societal challenges.

- Academic and Industry Research Collaborations: Bridging the gap between academic research and industry application is vital for innovation. Joint research initiatives and knowledge-sharing platforms can facilitate this exchange.

- **Engagement with Civil Society:** Including civil society in AI governance processes ensures diverse perspectives are considered, enhancing societal trust in AI technologies. Public consultations, AI literacy initiatives, and inclusive policy-making processes are key strategies.

Addressing these challenges requires a coordinated effort across all sectors of society. By fostering an ecosystem that encourages innovation while ensuring ethical, inclusive, and sustainable practices, we can harness the transformative potential of AI 2.0 for global benefit.

As we conclude this section and move towards wrapping up our report with a Conclusion and Recommendations, we will summarize key findings and propose strategic actions for stakeholders navigating the era of AI 2.0.

As we approach the conclusion of our report on AI 2.0 and its transformative potential, this final section will summarize our key findings and offer strategic recommendations for stakeholders. These recommendations aim to guide the responsible development, deployment, and governance of AI 2.0 technologies, ensuring their benefits are maximized while challenges are effectively addressed.

Conclusion and Recommendations

Summary of Key Findings

- Technological Foundations: AI 2.0, built on advancements in machine learning, deep learning, and big data analytics, represents a significant leap over its predecessor, enabling more complex, adaptable, and autonomous AI systems.

- Impact on Industries: Across healthcare, finance, manufacturing, and transportation, AI 2.0 offers unprecedented opportunities for efficiency gains, innovation, and addressing longstanding challenges.

- Societal Implications: The deployment of AI 2.0 technologies raises important considerations regarding employment, privacy, ethical use, and global inequalities, necessitating thoughtful dialogue and action.

- Economic Potential: With the capacity to significantly boost global productivity and innovation, AI 2.0 is projected to be a major economic force, potentially contributing up to $100 trillion to the global economy.

- Challenges and Solutions: Overcoming technical hurdles, navigating regulatory landscapes, and fostering collaboration among stakeholders are crucial steps towards realizing AI 2.0's full potential responsibly.

Strategic Recommendations

For Governments:

- Develop and implement clear, consistent regulatory frameworks that encourage innovation while protecting individual rights and promoting ethical AI use.

- Invest in digital infrastructure and education to prepare the workforce for an AI-driven economy and ensure equitable access to AI benefits.

• Foster public-private partnerships to leverage AI in addressing societal challenges, such as healthcare, education, and climate change.

For Industry:

• Prioritize the development of ethical, transparent, and inclusive AI technologies, incorporating diverse datasets and perspectives to mitigate biases.

- Invest in research and development while engaging in collaborations with academia to accelerate innovation and the application of AI 2.0 technologies.

- Implement robust data governance and cybersecurity measures to protect against breaches and ensure the trustworthiness of AI systems.

For Academia:

- Continue advancing AI research, focusing on addressing current limitations around efficiency, reliability, and ethical considerations.

- Strengthen partnerships with industry and government to facilitate the translation of research findings into practical applications and policies.

- Enhance interdisciplinary AI education programs to prepare the next generation of AI practitioners and researchers.

For Civil Society:

- Engage actively in the AI governance process, ensuring that diverse voices are heard and that AI development aligns with societal values and needs.

- Advocate for transparency, accountability, and inclusiveness in AI deployment and use, raising awareness of potential ethical and social implications.

- Support initiatives aimed at increasing digital literacy and understanding of AI among the general public.

AI 2.0 holds the promise to redefine the future, offering solutions to some of the most pressing global challenges while driving economic growth and innovation. However, realizing this promise requires a concerted effort from all sectors of society to navigate the accompanying challenges with foresight and responsibility. By adhering to the recommendations outlined in this report, stakeholders can work together to ensure that AI 2.0 fulfills its transformative potential in a manner that benefits humanity as a whole.

(Bonus)

For those who want to make money with Ai.

The Ai bundle - https://tinyurl.com/yp63c858

(Bonus 2)

Try Ai to redesign your whole entire house with this New simple software check it out here

Homedesigns Ai - https://tinyurl.com/3b3vyr73

www.ingramcontent.com/pod-product-compliance
Lightning Source LLC
Chambersburg PA
CBHW030049230526
45471CB00003B/1017